AND THE SEA

AND THE SEA

Poems

Christopher Buckley

THE SHEEP MEADOW PRESS
RIVERDALE-ON-HUDSON

All inquiries and permission requests should be addressed to:
The Sheep Meadow Press
P.O. Box 1345
Riverdale-on-Hudson, NY 10471

Designed and typeset by The Sheep Meadow Press.
Distributed by The University Press of New England.

Printed on acid-free paper in the United States. This book meets the guidelines for permanence and durability of the Committee on Production Guidelines for Book Longevity of the Council on Library Resources.

Library of Congress Cataloging-in-Publication Data

Buckley, Christopher, 1948-
--and the sea / Christopher Buckley.
    p. cm.
  ISBN 1-931357-33-1 (alk. paper)
  I. Title.
PS3552.U339A53 2006
813'.54--dc22

ACKNOWLEDGMENTS:

Grateful acknowledgment is made to the editors of the following publications, in which the original versions of these poems first appeared.

5 AM: All Saints' Day
Agenda: Floating
American Poetry Review: Loyalty; Mystery
Artful Dodge: Philosophy
Art/Life: Analects of the Essenes
Askew: Grey Evenings; Teleology
Boxcar: The Philosophy Professor Facing Retirement
The Café Review: Wooden Boats
Denver Quarterly: Travel; Prayer, Late Winter
The Georgia Review: Photograph of Pablo Neruda, Chile 1948/
    Photograph of the author, Eureka, CA 1948
Hotel Amerika: The Sea Again; My History of Ancient Egypt
Hubbub: Prophecy
Kestrel: Poem Beginning With a Line from Tu Fu
Poetry International: Catechism of the Sea
POOL: Waking Up in My Car at Miramar Point
Quarterly West: All But Lost
Redactions: Photograph of John Berryman on the Back of *Love*
    & Fame
Red Wheelbarrow: September
Runes: A Review of Poetry: Memory
Snake Nation Review: Spring Sabbatical
The Southeast Review: Apologia Pro Vita Sua
Tar River Poetry: Photo Without Cap
Terminus: My Parents' Photographs
Two Rivers Review: Entropy

Thanks to Nadya Brown for continued support and understanding; to Gary Soto for long-time friendship and support; and to Gary Young and Jon Veinberg for tireless editing and revision suggestions.

CONTENTS

IV.

V.

What is to become of us?
The sea, that has no ending,
is lapping at our feet.

—Stanley Kunitz
The Sea That Has No Ending

I

MEMORY

The fish's soul
　　　　　is his empty bones.
　　　　　–Yehuda Amichai

On that shore—driftwood, empty bones bumping
　　　　　up against rocks, low-tide beneath
a lace-window sky, a ribbed articulation of clouds
　　　　　at the edges, sparing us nothing, as forecast,
in the way of regret. We would lie then along the cloud-
　　　　　grey sand, in our cool unconscious youth,
in the overhanging bruises of the eucalyptus, our eyes
　　　　　filling with the watery apparatus
of the abstract and washed-out blue, day-dreaming
　　　　　through the daffodil light of Judy Holliday
in "Bells Are Ringing" or Sandra Dee in "A Summer Place."
　　　　　We didn't have the first idea about ideas,
and, diving beneath kelp beds, shot the carefree fish
　　　　　with our hand-sling spears and never gave
a thought to what the trident symbolized—a soul
　　　　　was only something in a catechism text,
an emptiness in the air we were never going to touch,
　　　　　unlike the eucharist-white bones of the fish.
And when the only bass I ever speared wriggled
　　　　　on the tines in the bright and awful air,
the slash in its side unfolded like bread soaked in wine,
　　　　　and its amber eye beheld me there and all the sky
could see who I was and had become with its ichor
　　　　　oozing on my sea-stained hands. And still
what sweet vowels the plovers and godwits sent up
　　　　　despite me in my frogman flippers and mask
that disguised so little as I thrust my stick and defied
　　　　　next to nothing in the sky. The gulls praised

the body of the world, and flew their grey rags of death,
        and loitered on the logs and seaweed there—
patient again as death—to see what I would do. And though
        wave after wave testified against me, I knew
no sorrow, and felt innocent as sea foam, unassailed
        as the blue-roofed bungalows of the resort,
the weekenders on the boardwalk, the ice plant
        over the seawall and the dunes. Everything
was, for the most part, unknown—the ridicule in the wind,
        the resurrection of dust, my spindrift breath,
and the ocean's churning roots—just driftwood bumping,
        beached forever—the sea wrack of the heart.

WAKING UP IN MY CAR AT MIRAMAR POINT

I was a child there, on the shore
    and the sea kept moving—
        I was sure it spoke

my name in the idiom of foam. I had
    a cloud imprinted on my forehead
        representing all I knew

and my soul's grey hands were knotted,
    anchored deeply beneath dark water
        like kelp struggling

toward the sun. I floated on the surface
    and drifted off somewhere bright
        and more remarkable where

I could not see to the heart of anything.
    But I learned to read the vanished
        lines of cypress, those shadows

edging the chalky cliffs. My work was to make
    something out of clouds, out of nothing
        more than the tide left behind,

than fell from the tablecloth of the blue
    and wonder why I'd ever abandon
        such a life? Skin diving,

surfing, I knew the salted margin of the air,
    the green intelligence of the sea,
        a second life in its spindrift

flesh, and studied the solitary physics of rain
  and light riding bare-backed and fish-
    fast through sun-sprays until

I was tumbled out in the booming soup like a leaf
  from a gale to float in across
    a quarter mile of rock

and shells out of range of any embrace. I came
  for the steady fusion of blood
    and oxygen, blue/red

beneath corpuscular space. I came and went,
  rode my motor bike away from town,
    and never saw the angels

in the mythical woods or alley ways—just the old
  men covering their heads in the sun,
    their handkerchiefs dabbing

at their brows, the sea gulls swaying in the air
  just beyond their benches. I was left
    with the impressionistic leaves,

the broken bits and silver left-overs of wind,
  with the high harmonics of the pines
    and eucalyptus in the last

inches of summer unthreaded through the palms,
  with stars that looked me in the eyes
    and the espionage of the breeze—

my impossible breath and the impossible universe,
  the sea that kept moving and
    left no memory of me.

WOODEN BOATS

Tierra del Fuego, Punta Arenas, Magellan,
Vasco de Gama, Juan Rodriquez Cabrillo,
or Gaspar de Portola—in 1958
I had all the answers
in Miss Vasquez's Geography Class.
I knew the New World as it was known,
as they declaimed it 400 years ago,
from their decks in San Diego, San Francisco,
the Bay of Monterey,
                    thinking
they knew all there was to know . . . .
But every 50 years a wind comes up
from nowhere, facts scuttle
like dry leaves on a pond,
and the universe changes again,
as, empty-headed before the sky,
we look down to our worthless notes
beneath the desk.
                    Now the invisible,
once impossible, sub-atomic particles
spin in theoretical defiance
of most every rule Einstein
put in the book.
                    And those tired souls
dragging back from work on the #26 bus,
the few silhouettes briefly before
the sea-green windows, they are all
we will likely know of illumination.
A heavy marine layer arrives each spring,
a full moon, dull as a trash can lid,
a lapsed atmosphere where we are

perhaps finally headed with our non-
essential salts and dust.

                  Romantics
still believe there is time to reaffix
the blue, to redefine the space
where we might find ourselves
reflected in the first bright dimension
of our dreams.

               So much has been
taken away while somewhere in the universe
no time has gone by at all . . . .
We recheck our charts about
the provinces and protectorates
of the past, the stalled longitude
of hope, and are left with nothing
that will help us homeward—
though we walk out each dawn
with the white clouds becalmed,
having claimed it all.

THERE

I've driven by a hundred times since the hundred times, early in the '60s, we parked along the shoreline for the twenty or thirty minutes of our permitted youth, our breath going nowhere beyond those steamed minutes on the windshield glass . . . or the fog, which sometimes sauntered in from the dark and held us there with no idea where we really were. . . . I remember the great black cypress leaning on the grey-black sky, and the moon going to pieces in the eternal branches, the soporific salt air rising off the lines of surf that had us dreaming down hill in that same spot with a view toward nothing but ourselves, awaiting the acceptable sublime. Alone there, a car or two wandering by in the dim world forty years ago. The white background music of the tide, the crush of stars, clichés, and unclear wishes extended beyond our curfew and the days to come—unseeable then as the islands off the seabeach at night, where we were bound to the star-brocaded waves, the beach fires smoldering in the on-shore air . . . . Let me see now, let me see . . . what great thing was it I was going out into the world to do, prepared only with my haircut and button-down blue oxford, my night-blind youth, buoyed, like the moon, by vague love in the great vague sky where I claimed to read the sea-scrawl scraps of light by all the certainty we had coursing our salt-warm blood at seventeen?

MY HISTORY OF ANCIENT EGYPT

The short version arrived in 1956 from Cecil B. De Mille, with Chuck Heston in his grey beard looking like Michelangelo, which is to say Moses, which is Art History 101, which I learned much later. In any event, God's coppery-green smoke snaked down out of the inky night over Luxor and found Yul Brynner's son and Pharaoh-to-be in the arc-lit stone palace and smothered him without a sound in Technicolor.

The under class greased the logs used to roll the pyramid stones, big as beer trucks, along the sandy streets, while Heston—due to some issues of class in connection to his birth—was demoted from the executive branch to dance in the mud pits and make bricks without straw. An administrative practice that quickly caught on.

There was a silent release in black&white, filmed near my home, in the Guadalupe Dunes, in 1923, with the obelisks and great pillared halls, parapets and lines of house-sized lions raised before the sea, which, once the sun set on the lower kingdom, eventually drove the sands in the direction of the past, covering all the plaster feet of the gods. These were finally left to the domain of the sun and waves to break to bits not that long after the caravans of Hollywood caterers got their panel trucks stuck for the last time in the reedy creek crossing leading out of there.

The re-release of The Ten Commandments in 1965 was the last movie, I think, that my girlfriend and I ever saw together, and since we had read the book in grammar school and knew the ending, we walked out on Yvonne de Carlo, Heston, and the whole lot just after the red sea parted like two giant waves at Waimea cresting in a Bruce Brown surf movie. We sat in my '59 Chevy and had a fight, no doubt precipitated by her stern, pharaoh-like father with his all but shaved head and his dictates about how often we could date, and time limits talking on the phone. I'd learned nothing from the ancients and the lost civilizations of the sand that could help me there;

in those days there were fewer places from which to summon plague on short order. For all I could see, the future looked like the past with improved transportation.

Later, one day in my mid 40s, I'd see Yul Brynner on TV doing a commercial for The National Cancer Society—I don't recall his surroundings—warning against smoking . . . more serious and earnest than he'd ever been, after he was dead.

SPRING SABBATICAL

Wind-strewn, the thin afternoon clouds string together a rib cage, the white and almost transparent vertebrae of the blue. I don't know what the wind wants now, running its fingers through new leaves of pomegranate and podocarpus, buddleia and rock rose in my green and overgrown garden. What did it ever want?

Hummingbirds are at the cape honeysuckle and madeira—what do they ask for but the thrumming and varied appreciations of light? And me—now that I have a few minutes to stare off into nothing? Wasn't this my first occupation, one for which I showed exceptional promise, daydreaming happily in the grey classrooms of long division and fractions, handwriting exercise books? I was assessing the progress of March clouds as they inched through the butter-bright tops of the acacias just beyond the great framed windows, clouds whose sky-scrawl resembled mine with my Shaeffer cartridge fountain pen-swirls and blots above the sun-blistered sandstone peaks.

And if I had a soul—as they kept insisting that I did—with its parochial obligations, with its invisible tallies of plus and minus, then I understood it only there, just out the high transom, in terms of clouds where I was drifting along, breathing unconsciously with everything I would ever be worth, naming the lost continents of the chalk-white, midday moon.

What wouldn't I have given to recall that ten years ago before the petty academic scrapping got to me and threw off the rhythm in my heart like a scratch, a skip in an old LP? What would I give to fully know this, this afternoon lying back beneath the patio umbrella on my dandy plastic chaise lounge—the spring geraniums vibrant against the air with their lipstick reds and pinks, the marigolds in their pots brilliant as a ring of suns around the calm blue neck of that

Hindu elephant god—something I would have easily believed back then.

The lawn already mowed and trimmed a week ago so I might come to this—30 minutes of mindless mid-afternoon reflection, dozing with my great grey cat sharing the lounge, nothing to do but look around and exhale evenly through the almost empty sky, letting my blood download its indiscriminate freight, making some lighter sense of things, doing no more finally than it seems I ever should have in the first place.

ALL BUT LOST

Here, as always, the bygones of childhood, heavy light
      and dust off the wings of birds I watched
          vanishing in the west

as I stepped out from the Saturday matinee—all of it
      languishing beyond all help. . . .
          We arrived ready

to accept any bright syllable from the waves, the alliteration
      of the tide underwriting our joy. For a time
          there was no past,

only the mid-day sun and sand burning the immediate
      soles of our feet—everything we knew
          of iniquity before floating

out on the green swells and foam—a semaphore of clouds
      lining the horizon, the abbreviations and
          conditional clauses of God

we could not decode beyond a blue distraction. Heart white
      as a Sunday shirt, and I learned close
          to nothing, and happily,

for years—the ratio in my bones between earth and sky
      leaning heavily to the invisible air where
          the clouds alone were the sky's

collateral—so much rummage now . . . the sparkling prayer-
      wheel of stars spinning away from us
          every night, and all of us

under stars. The strategy of the sea is to live with its losses,
      the dark sea, all but lost in this poem.
            But who cares what

we know now—ancient ballast of salt sinking in our veins
      where the sea sounded back the first
            oath of light to let us be?

II

LOYALTY

My father knew next to nothing, really,
        about how to live this life—
business partners stole him blind;
        he had no friends and never
drank. Even Jean Paul Sartre could get
        sentimental after three martinis
and some saxophone music, but my father
        was serious about advertising,
knew the fix was in on the network news,
        all the professors were communist
dupes. But he maintained a clear affection
        for the abstract theme of stars,
always taking a minute to point overhead
        to the beamy sky in Montecito,
long before the '60s and all our industrial
        radiance and silt clouded our clear
view outward. He'd talk about space—flying
        saucers, life on other worlds, time
disappearing at the speed of light, whirligigs
        and flywheels of the cosmos that
assumed significance for him, an intangible
        but bona fide machinery reflecting us . . . .
He pledged allegiance to the vast unknown—
        yet another thing he was somehow
smugly sure he was certain of. I had been
        drilled by the forbidding priests
and nuns, and one take on the dim and indefinite
        to me seemed as valid as the next.
But he discerned no conspiracy in the stars,
        no secret in the silvered edge
of air that would not save us from the burden

of the dark. I was seven, or eight,
and on the swings each day at school flew
        upside down in the blue cup
of the world, and it was all the same to me
        as I pulled the sky through my lungs
and scanned the enjambed grey line of clouds
        for any lost music, any foundation
for the casual delight that must have been
        taken in the seas set spinning,
in the collective fidelity of our hearts, here
        in the middle distance from the sun.

The trees of my childhood shook their heads
        as I outdistanced myself with
speculation—alone with the wind's thin strings,
        believing I saw the light
of our souls floating on the coattails
        of a storm, or in the white caps'
salt dust. And mornings now I catch myself
        complaining with the finches
in a buddleia bush, with the brigade of starlings
        who have something persistent
to say about who will inherit the earth.
        Again today, I want to write something
without clouds in it, without loss, without whatever
        it was that the wind blew through
without a trace, engaged as I am in devotion,
        in subterfuge on my own behalf.
My father who was burned back to star dust
        and scattered over the sea.

PHILOSOPHY

For Luis Omar Salinas

Walking back and forth in mist, side-stepping
    the haphazard tide, he selects

a sand dollar, shakes out the insignificant music
    of sand, an echo of the sky.

Picking up beach glass, he recalls an obscure glow,
    the dulled parameters of the past,

and looks to the unresolved whitecaps off shore,
    fragments of this world catching,

perhaps, the light of another . . . . He might be
    recalling his college texts,

pages open to the wind each spring, to France and
    Albert Camus and company doubting

the underpinnings of existence, questioning why
    we might stand with anything

more than an impromptu purpose before the empty
    reiterations of waves . . . all so much

self-indulgence, as they rummaged comfortably around
    in their tilted berets, café to café,

depressed in their stoic sentences. For all of that,
    the gulls appear to sustain some

ontological concerns above the bins, and now no clouds
        oppose him; it is clear all the way

to heaven, and despite the poverties of wind, some
        unequivocal beauty breaks out

among surviving lemon groves. But on the grey
        reaches of the shore, he has always

been old, shuffling by the diminished cries of bathers
        in the surf, the broken cabanas

with an intrinsic romantic tilt—such sea-dust
        as a heart never fully overthrows.

Black birds whistle across the vacant parking lot,
        and now it doesn't seem to matter

that the sky won't listen, that not a soul is prepared
        as he begins to address the palms.

MYSTERY

Emptiness is not near what you thought it might be—
      the small bones the sky

has left you where the sea passed by, the salt
      air drying on your skin,

a skein thin and transparent as the maps
      to the lost mines of Namibia.

You have been rag-picking among the clouds
      again, staring off into space,

white tattoos dissolving like clues, like sea-
      thumbed chips of light.

And now, in their dark robes, the starlings
      conspire on the phone lines

as if they might, any minute, give in to the intrigue
      of evening, and vanish. I sit here

on the side of the birds, in the custody of dusk,
      overlooking the cliff, examining

the evidence of chalk—all the crumbling exoskeletons
      organized at our fingertips

so we might uncover the matter of light, diagram
      its waves and speed against

the black-board of space, and know our place,
        and time. God knows who we are,

knows each forgotten breath. And I have suffered
        no more than the next one. Still, our

convictions don't add up, some arithmetic missing
        since day one—clusters of galaxies,

of greasewood, carbon dating, the silent witnessing
        of the Himalayas. Each evening, the fog

covers up the coast, the shore disappears into the grey,
        into another world—as likely as not

the same thing. The salt, the dust, the old
        suspects—I continue to have them

change hats and coats for this, for any scrap
        of evidence we have of heaven.

POEM BEGINNING WITH A LINE FROM TU FU

Soon now, in the winter dawn,

                                      I will face my 55th year.

I don't know that life goes anywhere,

                               really,

but thinking back on it

                      in the moment

it takes another leaf to fall,

                      I see how many more

evenings I've needed

                      sitting out here

letting the wind pass calmly

                            through my hands,

overlooking

               the star pines, and jacarandas,

the valley of home . . .

                     I think of the friends

of my youth,

               Montecito and the sea—

                          green hills,

that have traveled off

                   without me now,

                           beyond even

the grinding optimism

                   of stars . . .

When I look at the brown haze

                       that hovers

between here

               and the channel islands,

I take an early drink,
                    and praise whatever is left
of my Fate—
                    no different finally,
                                        than anyone else's . . .
I have no idea what
                    I want now
                                        beyond everything
I've ever had,
                    all over again
                                        and the legs to withstand
the long-term
                    effects of gravity,
                                        continuing
to have their way with me,
                    pulling me back
                                        into myself
like a disused star
                    that will one day implode,
                                        invisibly
compress beyond the heart,
                                        and somehow withstand
the heavens . . . .

                    The wind comes
                                        from 10,000 miles away,
the sweet air
                    lifts the atoms of light.
                                        One thin cloud,
                                                            shaped
like a soul,
                    is back-lit, briefly,
                                        by the moon.
Whenever I can,
                    I stare off into space

    26

                                        as if something
more than the resin of pines,
                        will come to me—
                                        the salt breeze,
rising over my head.
                        I watch
                                the small shore birds,
their tracks unthreading
                        back and forth
                                        before the tide . . .

ANALECTS OF THE ESSENES

As little as rain matters to the sea, as much as dust
     Spun up into clouds—we are substantial as the sky
       Above the clouds, all it refuses to reveal.

The tent ripples with the indeterminate names of wind,
     Reminders of the distance between breath and air,
       Between sand and salt on the tongue.

Thorn trees send up their green thoughts, the last stars
     Sleep, and we sing the firmament, the constellations
       Clustered in the dark, the dim memory

Of a heart as the sparks retrace the routes that fuse
     Our hands held up each dawn—sunlight spooled
       Behind closed eyes where we still see distant

Walls aflame. What was given to us for safekeeping
     Smolders in the dark, but who would set foot
       Beyond darkness only to change

The habit of suffering? We must walk over stones,
     Along cliffs that sift away in chalk, before
       The world, in its splendor, descends on us.

At evening, I can trace the gold thread edging the hills
     Between here and heaven—and I cannot say
       There will ever be less suffering . . . .

Water lines on rock, the dry blood and breath of urns,
     The unanswered interrogative of the sky—God
       Can be seen as a white sail slipping over

The sea, the water its own eternity beyond the shaking
Faith of trees. A star burning above the voices
Of the palms, the blurred scrolls of dawn.

ALL SAINTS' DAY

I'm nodding off beneath
the ornamental plum,
its dark leaves lifting
now and then in a bright
gust, like song notes
on the blue . . . .
     My cat
stretches out with me
on our white recliner,
and the sun hovers
above the autumn garden,
hummingbirds dog-fighting
in a blur about the feeder.
Our neighbor's persimmons
shimmer above the fence—
a gold orrery spinning
in place, suspended
in the still afternoon
alongside my grey cats,
my grey heart, and
the thick and almost visible
ascension of the air.
     Soon,
I will break open
a pomegranate from our bush,
eat its jewel-red encomiums
and know it's sufficient
to simply gaze about
the burnished yard,
and like the bees praise
everything at hand before

30

it falls . . . .
       All I need
is time, a long lasting
bit of it beyond
the shadow-heavy roofs
where the birds gather
at this same hour each day—
starlings, scrub jays, doves—
for the last striations and
instructions of the light,
which are theirs forever . . . .

CATECHISM OF THE SEA

> With a premonition of light the sea sang.
> —Octavio Paz

In those days, we accepted the spray,
    the glitter off the wings

Of the drifting birds as the bright
    evidence of life everlasting.

Corroboration arrived in the alliteration
    of waves, a tender star or two

Clinging to the tassel-ends of heaven,
    a cloud, light as our paper souls,

Cleaned and pressed like a Sunday suit. We were
    given to the immaculate sands,

The incomparable charity of the sky,
    and in autumn, only minor

Disruptions of dust spun up at street corners,
    the glint from mica and the foil

Of gum wrappers causing us to momentarily
    close our eyes—as close as we came

To death, unrecognized there or in the storm
    troughs spiking a slate-dark sea.

Our hearts were white as our uniform shirts,
    as the wild fields of alyssum,

And I learned nothing of set theory and equations
    scrawled across the blackboards,

Was sent out to clap erasers, returning with the unequal
    properties of silence and covered

In a veil of powdered chalk, happily, for years, taken
    as I was with the wobbly grandeur

Of the blue. Now, so much lost, so much taken away
    with the absolute gravity, grind,

Spin and brine of every invisible law, phrases
    fly out the window to no one,

More darkness recited among the stars.
    Whatever I've been talking about

No longer seems to be the point—the ocean,
    can't breathe, the revisions

Of the past will never save us now. It's all
    a fog inside me, refusing to burn off,

To offer up the rote responses to the choruses
    of salt testifying to nothing,

The nonsense it all comes to like the first
    day of summer and school reports

For science torn from my binder and tossed
    onto the winds, so help me.

Now alone, I see the clouds under sail,
    embarking out there for a port

Where the air ends, where all that waits
        for us is the heavy ringing of

The sea's dull bells. Pick any five men
        mumbling in their coats, drifting

On the cliff-side benches, an on-shore breeze
        at their unmetaphysical throats,

And see how many words of allegiance or joy
        can be squeezed out at this late date.

Make something of the one palm tree whose green
        fronds are comparatively glorious

And resist the graceless rip and under-tow—
        it's just that way with God.

III

PHOTOGRAPH OF PABLO NERUDA, CHILE, 1948/ PHOTOGRAPH OF THE AUTHOR, EUREKA, CA, 1948

> The smell of barber shops makes me break out sobbing.
> —Pablo Neruda

Old comrade, who needs a barber shop now?
Not me. And not you in 1948—the year
I was born, the year you were almost
already bald and most of who you would become—
except that it calls back a lost world
of Violet Water and Tres Flores, Lucky Tiger
and Bay Rum—a blameless childhood
savoring the glassy syllables
of the surf . . . .
                    What dreams were left
on the lips of the wind as you looked out
on the tender seas, on clouds that skimmed
the Pacific of nostalgia for the next 55 years
since this grainy snap, since you last thought
of a haircut?
                    Sea-gypsies like ourselves
treasure whatever is thrown back by the tide,
each blurred chip of beach glass revealing
a misplaced scrap of light. We reclaim
that world dreaming of Vitalis, and Aqua Velva—
clippers humming behind our ears, thinning
shears clicking below the barbicide
in tall sea-tinged jars, talc descending
like cloud dust, and that blossom of alcohol,
mist of bloated roses, musty newspapers
and politics, standing chrome ashtrays
filled with sand, the stubs of White Owls,
Dutch Masters, and Muriel panatelas.
Argosy, LIFE, or the *Saturday Evening Post*

in the lap of an old-timer dozing
in the chair next to the john . . .
the slow blades of a ceiling fan churning flies
and the worlds we were losing in Temuco
and Montecito . . . .
                    You escaped on horseback
over the Andes, to Europe. I rode in comfortably
on the coattails of post-war economic recovery
on the northern California coast,
bald as a grape in my parents' baby pictures,
as you on your dust jacket photos . . . .
There I am, propped up and happy on the hood
of their new Pontiac, wearing a cap
the same as you'd wear the next 25 years,
and knowing, like you, the sound of the sea
before I knew my name, and 20 years to come
before I'd know yours . . . .
                    Nevertheless,
here we are, preserved for posterity, the proletariat,
the glossy, on-going promotion of dust—you looking
young in middle age, younger than I've ever seen you,
younger than I am now—
                    sand-colored snapshot,
your short, steel-wool beard, the worker's shirt
and insubordinate look of a defender
of the oil-drowned seas, the clear-cut trees,
of the right of miners, of shovelers of nitrate
to sip at the honeycomb of oxygen—for which
they ran you out of the dining rooms of *caballeros*,
out of the Senate, for which they ate
their own words when yours made them infamous.
A few decades—out and back—*saludos*, and
adios.
        These photos recall that sleep-walking world
before each place was injured and improved,

before we were left with just snips of memory,
dreaming on opposite sides of the sky,
where there are no barber shops, no seats
in the cinema on Saturday afternoons,
no double feature and world news in black and white,
no wind-combed beaches reflecting the clear
thinking of the clouds.
                    I never knew you
looked like this—hard, rough, defiant
as a root, spinning in place with the fury
of a water spout. I only knew the image
of a clean shaven, avuncular poet, bald
as a pope, but someone with rip tides,
the raging syntax of the ocean
up his sleeve.
                    Who were we all our lives
ago, there on the edge of the sea,
the sky giving back our untroubled visions
in tide pools, in the resinous stanzas
of the pines? The fair weather clouds
floating our hearts as we headed off to school
each morning, stepping from stone to stone
on a path to the sky, where deep in the anonymity
of the air, we first and briefly were
whoever it was we said we were, Neftali Reyes!

G. DE CHIRICO AT EAST BEACH, SANTA BARBARA, 1973

The day dissolves into an imperial blue—behind me,
the square where the overhead train steams by

and the shadow of the municipal tower, remain unmoved.

The sun is fixed behind the architecture of trees,
the sky rustles, as always, when the birds depart,

and I am at home with the spindrift displayed

upon the wind. A Phoenician sail still asleep
and motionless in the distance, a turquoise sea bruised

with black and fiery flecks—that was childhood.

But the tailor's chalk marks are still inside my chest.
At this point, nothing will change

the deep perspective, the loose scaffolding of the past. . . .

The fog starts in, and a crow in a palm is not an emblem
of anything beyond the air—images of the ordinary

world are as close as we will come. Nonetheless,

the ocean abandons us to ourselves and a nostalgia
for the infinite, the incontestable limbo of the swells

until we ask nothing of the thick and untranslatable

log book of light. My heart has its blue
constructions, its unlikely dreams, dim as dishwater

by comparison here—now, memories desert my mind

like a handful of clouds making for the horizon, also dreaming . . . .
Sooner or later waves will cast us out

and we'll be called to interpret our dreams,

shining or grey among the rusting infrastructure
of the years—only fragments to fall back on

and explain ourselves by. The salt breeze stings

my eyes, and the enigma of another autumn afternoon
stations itself above my heart—today, the only clue

I have is God's red glove, nailed to a wall.

MY PARENTS' PHOTOGRAPHS

Who knew I looked like Pablo Neruda
in 1948, years before he would? But
in one of my parents' baby pictures,
above the Pacific and Humboldt Bay,
bald as a pope, or wearing that same
cap he'd later wear, I'm propped up on
the hood of their cloud-colored Pontiac,
arms spread out to each side as if
blessing the air, learning my balance
for the years of surfing to come, or
wondering what my chances were of
lifting off into the rising wind with
the few syllables at my command, in
a wide-eyed and under-exposed joy.

Here's a boy, his happy hair slicked
back with Wildroot Cream Oil in 1952.
His mother and Aunt have taken him
to the Cincinnati Zoo; he's oblivious
to his matching home-made floral
shirt and shorts, his ridiculous white
as Ivory Soap Flakes, Hollywood sun-
glasses. And for no apparent reason,
he's still grinning out of the grey
light of this wallet-sized snap.

★ ★ ★

Already now, I am old enough
for my mother to be passing on
her photos—a practical matter,
I suppose, as, nearing 80, there's

no one else . . . but how do you
look past the light dissolving
at the corners, the black &
white despair that has gathered
all this time like the dull and
distant clouds in the corner
of this one above her childhood
farmhouse? A book of absence,
the specific gravity of loss.

Among them her umber, studio-
softened portrait—an RN during
the war—bangs like Bette Davis,
a flip like a dozen other stars;
it was auburn, as they said then.
And how young and harmless
she and my father both look
in color Christmas cards with me
and our Irish Setter, there on
Miramar beach before everyone
had heard about Santa Barbara,
and anyone could live there.

★   ★   ★

Before that we'd moved east when my father
finished school and found a job. In this one,
I'm 3, and despite a grey West Virginia January
afternoon, and to escape our dingy apartment
a few blocks from the decent one my father
was refused because he had a child—(though
he looked the woman straight in the face and
offered to drive to the river, drown the child,
and return in 15 minutes)—I'm outside, posed

on the cement steps beside my birthday cake.
My father unfolds the Kodak and shoots as I
sit still as the part in my hair. I look pleased
though I'm in a raincoat that comes to my knees
and wearing stiff white leather toddler shoes,
because the cake is big with white Crisco
frosting and red sugar roses—pleased when
my father calls me "Crisco," though it's grey
and grainy all about us in this 8 x 10, where
my coat and cap and I match the grizzled
atmosphere of Charleston. For what it's worth,
I have yet to begin looking up to the sky.

And I'm happy for one the size of 4 postage stamps,
taken inside the farm house . . . I can barely see to
climb into that wedge of light in my grandfather's lap
as he sits in his Morris Recliner, in his tan Dickey
shirt and trousers, his retired farmer's uniform.
I am 2 or 3, wearing shorts, sheared for summer,
and so our half-bald heads shine together. Then
one I never saw—grandfather and grandmother standing
alone on a Florida beach, late '40s or'50s; he's wearing
a dark pin-striped suit and Panama hat; she's posed
in a flowered dress, in her high black lace shoes,
pressing a modest bonnet with one hand to her head.
They've been to church or out to Sunday supper, as
dressed up as they will ever be. They are floating,
surrounded by an amber haze, the beach stretches
away in a cloud . . . I think I see a dusting of flour
on her cheek-she pulls the stool up to the kitchen
counter and hands me a water glass so I can press
biscuits, white as sea light, from the dough . . . .

44

My father's are sadder. Not for the blur and rusty
pallor from his mother's time, the stiff Edwardian
posing with her sister turn of the century—1900—
the one no one cares about any more. My father, 3
in this '20s-sepia haze with ivory borders, wears
a pith helmet and uncharacteristic grin in the jungle
of backyard Ohio. Here's my grandfather Lon with my
waif-like father in their '30s caps and knickerbockers
at Niagara Falls, a once-in-a-lifetime opportunity, a place
I only saw on boxes of '50s Shredded Wheat. Or several
of the columns and two-story imperial high school.
And beneath the ionic capitals, I barely recognize
my father in his graduation gown and mortar board,
the modest scholar he would never really become.

Then in an air cadet uniform, outbreak of the war,
all that small town significance—all of our relatives
soon gone—Uncle Charlie who lived in a hotel, and
Bernie who drove by each night for beer, Aunt Babe,
straw-thin in her bones even then—on the cement
porch of the big house you could buy back then for
a handshake and a few dollars down in the middle
of America, in a place like Washington Court House,
Ohio. Flip forward 50 years, after my father's death,
I'm handed a box with photos and an empty billfold,
and there is one packet from the drug store, labeled
in ball point pen, simply "home." No relatives, none
of my grandparents or their white slat-board house,
no statues, street signs or faithful dogs, but just color

45

print after color print of the town in the first glories
of autumn, the town he came back to only once, late,
I think, in the '70s. He took the train cross-country,
having stepped off a plane state-side after the war,
having piloted DC-3s Cairo to Brazil, re-fueling in
the south Atlantic, on that dot of rock, Ascension Island,
having lost his only friend in the world, Howard, on his
last day as a flight instructor. He vowed never to get in
a plane again—not to go home, not to see his mother alive
or dead. But that last visit, took his last snaps around
the town, the blazing gold and burnt sienna, the crimson

rush of leaves and air, of parks, the Indian burial
mounds all in Kodachrome prints—trees everywhere
as in that vanished garden you carry with you always,
no matter where you live . . . . No people, just that
burning past living in softened Technicolor where
you most likely will never go again. All these things
so fixed and heavy with light, and gone, that wreck
your heart and never save you in the end. Packets
of the past you pass along to children, if you have
children, and if not, put away and try to not,
with the dark inching closer, ever look at again . . . .

★   ★   ★

I don't know what to make of a dream
the other night—my father kissing me
on the cheek as he never did in life,
not decked-out in the coffee-colored suit
and knit tie of his spiffy college snaps.
For his penance, I suppose, he must wear
shabby clothes from some metaphysical
Thrift—trousers cuffed too short, tattered
coat, padding leaking out the shoulder

seam so perhaps he might know,
learn at last, what mattered here, if far
too late for the little left in an envelope
of prints. All of it so long ago, and yet
by some accounts, no more than a blink
or two of light passing through the earth.
Whatever the coordinates of loss—dreams,
3 x 5s, 8 x 10s, sun-glint on the sea—each
image we hold up is an enlarged silence,
cloud forms, ashes shifting, losing shape—
a coincidence of the light we briefly were.

PHOTOGRAPH OF JOHN BERRYMAN ON THE BACK OF *LOVE & FAME*

> I have no idea whether we live again.
> –John Berryman

I see the man who wrote his 11 intemperate letters
to the Lord is the man half grateful near his end,
a man almost at ease and deep behind his whiskers here.
A charmer who won't be completely run to ground,

grizzled as the granite going to pieces at his back,
he's channeling his last cloud-split reasoning
directly at the doubtful sky, uncovering any worth
or last ditch redeeming chance, and carefully

subscribing to that. Who then knows about the soul-
chipped away with age, grey with cosmic grit,
some evanescent paste holding together beyond
our bones? I have some interest in this late line

of questioning, that desperate dodge and grab at
conviction while balancing on one foot, the sinking
weight of everything you likely know on the other.
I have a friend who revered and loved the man, as,

I imagine, God intended us to respect that knot
of light burning in the rare and fervent few among us.
33 years ago, Berryman posed, nonchalant
before the lens in Ireland—Latinate, distilled,

high lonesome and jazzy riffs mixed with reflex
and a syntactic ear for idiosyncrasy, inward
somnambulism—a sober self-estimate that held him
steady amid the wobbling flames, dreaming

in the distracted atmosphere with love and fame
trailing a ways off from where he later waved
then stepped away, dawdling toward the glory
of the dust. For a man who could not much love

himself he came generous with his love and trust
at last in God. O, time wears us away to little
more than salt or sea air, here or elsewhere, but how
to know which metaphysical hammerlock's going

to pin us down the years and force capitulation?
Yet, he's still credible, walking the edge, a famous
sparkle of doubt in the eyes, teetering in the blind
up-drafts of belief-both sides of the street in play,

sand beneath the soft soles of his feet. He expects
to fall and will blame, ex post facto and no doubt
rightly, logically so, God, when he is not there,
to swoosh out of the unphysical aether to hold,

metaphorically, his hand, in His infinite one,
that ardent strophe of flesh and blood above
the common traffic of the world, where sooner or
later all our blood and bony minds fall to wreck,

one afternoon. One day to the next, I find myself
as reasonably sure as Berryman about the afterlife,
and I would, at 50-something, line up behind him,
my right hand raised into the air in hope of one.

But my heart's not finally in it; it's still half bitter
like a root vegetable they always said was good
for you, and so will not likely lift me, heavy out
of this world, as his must have—singing, praising

purely the fog-thick invisible source, the blind-
spot in creation sustained by desperate lines,
and he dead-grateful for his gift, disavowing
eloquence alone. Yet somehow he firmly clutched

in one mildly shaking hand a glass half-full of Faith.
For any proof, I have only, as I said, the friend who
knew him, this photo, his clipped and thorny song—
the conflicted pledges of an absent minded God . . . .

PHOTO WITHOUT CAP

I am not so bald as Paul Cézanne
in 1880, in one of his 30 self-portraits—
but our cheeks are both thick and flushed,
foreheads expanding with sunlight.
He builds a face with blocks of terra cotta,
volume and modulations demonstrating
its geometry against the background—
at my age, they are all on the same level
of interest. For the psychological record,
the dark, expressionless eyes are something
you recognize when you keep looking
for explanations beyond the shifting
of your reflection in shop windows,
in the morning mirror, combing what hair
there's left. Of course, no one compares
himself to Cézanne, but I feel camaraderie
in the humility of his uncovered scalp,
in the hatched brush strokes of age—
a dry landscape at your back, a few sticks
representing themselves in a place as plain
as Lompoc, more than a few degrees of bucolic
separation from *Jas de Bouffan*. And
just like Cézanne, I am dissolving
into the dust and dissipating light,
into the water-color shade of poplars,
or the rain beneath the lime tree,
registering last impressions of the world.
If I believe the information of my eyes,
I see that I was given all I deserved—
lemons blazing in the trees, trumpet vines
the colors of flesh and blood, the afternoon sky
turning white in relief against all our desires

which come back each evening like crows
into the grove of pines—the air polished
with sea mist, salt. Old as I am, what could
there possibly be worth lying about now?
Unlike God, we have few disguises—finally,
we are so many minerals, so there was no reason
for my cap in this photo—I am as much at risk
as the trees under the sky, lost in thought.
There is a river behind me, carrying off
everything into the empty horizon.
Each time I inhale, the earth has me
by the lungs, by those bound internal wings—
another man with measured breath and days
invisibly counted out in the cold and blue
landscape of release and resignation.

IV

GREY EVENINGS

He vivido sin ti, mi Dios, pues no ayudaste
Esta incredulidad que hizo triste me alma.
            —Luis Cernuda

Sea mist, and the sparkling stars go dim—God wearing an old shirt,
        they say, so no one will notice when he comes to check.
            2/3ds of my life gone, but I'm still

punching, yet it's easy to feel that you're on the ropes, that
        no matter what, the fix is in, here on the edge
            of the sea, staring off above the earth,

directing the sum of your discontent at a heaven vague beyond
        distance and belief. Here's the wind again with its
            tract on solitude, the hard facts

of the flesh. Like a sleep walker, my arms embrace the air—
        on my toes all this time, and I almost understand. . .
            much the way, at Five air escaped

with a gasp into air as I unwound the metal strip around
        a can of tennis balls, and I only half puzzled
            at the invisible forces before me,

believing then in the communion of saints, there reliably, above
        the blooming jacaranda boughs shading the courts
            in Manning Park. Tonight, equally as removed,

as blue, stars will gather above the hills of Montecito where
        I'll never find my way back. Behold—as they used to say—
            the pale evening, the grey silhouette

of Eden. No wonder a little light has an inexhaustible hold on us.
But it is not infinite; we have language that explains it,
that excuses us with a gouache

of coastal clouds deepening the brief paragraph of dusk.
My oak desk is a diary of worms. The streets,
the black grease spots of memory,

slide away in ellipses. . . the horizon dull as an albumin print
where everything is indistinct, veiled, impenetrable
finally, as my father's ghost-white hair

in those tiny negatives from the '40s, as the old school house,
the vista from the foothills from where we went
nowhere fast to find ourselves

apostates in the cathedral of the sea—the blood-warm water,
the empirical tides. Who ever prayed, "World
without end, Amen," surely meant it,

but didn't have the first idea . . . . Now we understand that
the slurries of stars are not just out the window
or running on pulleys across

a crystal vault. But where are they, really? Or are we,
for that matter, with every holy, glowing, cosmic
object blasted and red-shifted away

from us toward nobody knows what? Which fragments of this
world, held up to the light, betray the outline
of another world beyond?

The sea has it both ways, and, given our primordial self-pity,
isn't saying—any glimmer of Paradise far behind us
in a fog. And somehow we had it coming. . . .

56

THE SEA AGAIN

The sky is anchored to your feet, the stands of eucalyptus moored against midnight; it doesn't look like anyone is going anywhere. Wake me in the dead of night, before I can clear my head of the dark swells, and ask me what I truly need. I will answer, A handful of birds, or, God Made Me—both are true. Western blue bird, sunset red breast, my arms empty but for the equivocating fabric of the air, the old notes always up there above us. We filter the present through our memories of the past, and, strictly speaking, we live there. Our brains take time to process what we think—the present happened some time ago.

Rote memory and the feedback loops to the pig-iron sentences in the Baltimore Catechism: Who Made You? Why Did He Make You? And I sang back the answers, but what I knew in my breath and in my blood was Kickball, Thistle, Oak Tree, Wave, and, as God himself would not appear, I accepted substitutions in the sky, and took in equal parts of oxygen and doubt.

Whatever the oceans once dreamed washes away or is flayed in the caucus of the sun. The fish can't breathe. No architecture of light, no revisionist history is going to change the now and the then. Nevertheless, my 56th winter, and any day is a good one. If the soul has a window, it looks out on spindrift, salt, our little life aimless as the old ostentation of the stars—the earth imperfect, eternal—the red planets and spiral galaxies rising up like orange peels on a dark tide.

I don't care, finally, if God is terrible, or vengeful, an old God. Let there be something sturdier than the sea of grasses, the diminished plains. Some days I think the waters turn white with His worry, some days with the torments we've invented. Who could blame Him, if He's grown disinterested, if He's given up? No matter what I think, I just hope there is some there, there—beyond the clouds, the waves, the shadows on the empty surface of the sea.

FLOATING

Slow, late afternoon clouds collide—the indolent motion of lilies
by a pond, a water snake, white music scored on phone lines,

time signatures in the corner of the sky, treble clef and bass—
half, whole, quarter notes, airy flags which compound

the cream-colored magnolia blossoms above the patio, the humming
birds, their lint-light bodies at the feeder, stilled a second

like the atmosphere, like the old sea-grey brine, circumspect and
awash about my brain. Aside from the hummers' sugar-engine thrum

the air is becalmed, and I recall a time when my one occupation
was to lie back among the foothill weeds and see what might

suggest itself in the sky, my thoughts as unrestrained as the airless
reach of angels' wings, their unapplied choirs and confidential harmonies.

Those days off from school my business was to forestall syntax,
the diagramming of the future tense, to stay afloat like cirrocumulus

at the vacant edge of heaven with nothing but the blank sheet
of my imagination, upon which, true to form then, I impressed

precious little . . . unlike the last 30 freighted years when there
has been little time to stretch out on the sun-bleached recliner

and sip from the brimming cup of the blue, praise the smoky, plum
blossom moon, the essential verses of emptiness—my breath teamed

with the teaming winds, the gift of air with which we first set forth
drifting happily down, overlooking the bright realms of dust.

PRAYER, LATE WINTER

Sun burning down in fog, Point Conception
      dissolving into the grey—as good
          a time as any to think

of another world. Nonetheless, I can still be found
      on my bench before the waves,
          each dark line

of breakers opening and closing on
      a darkness beyond which
          I don't know what . . .

The sea is still deaf; nothing intercedes
      for us no matter how long we bring
          our petitions here.

And by now I am also aware that the sky
      is irretrievable, like the past—
          it isn't anybody's.

But I go along with the seabirds and agree
      that we should keep moving
          as long as we can.

Again this year the rains will be heartless
      over the solemn boulevards.
          And in the empty

galleries of wind, who will know who
      I really am, having barely survived
          the needless deaths

of the night-blooming jasmine, the ship-wrecked
    moons on our mountain range? I look back—
        each breath a tributary

to the ambiguous clouds. How was it that I ever
    felt God was traveling with me,
        or hidden just behind

the inarticulations of the air? So long, so far
    removed, what can be expected
        of our forsaken voices?

A consolation of birds stitches the edge
    of evening—I'm willing now to let them
        have the last labored words.

AUGUST MOON

3 am, walking the hall again,
back yard flooded with light,
and the days floating there
like smoke from old party lanterns
hung in the trees.
                    It's nothing
to say everything on earth
is related to everything
on earth—but how foolish
we have been to act otherwise
all this time . . . .
                    So it could be
Li Po's cricket singing
in this obscure hour, and if not to me,
to whom? Perhaps to Lizzie,
my Russian Blue, who listens
at the window, then climbs back
to her corner of the bed?
                        My 55th summer
and beyond the cricket's song,
the many stars, the many possibilities
flying past us—and now my blood
feels dull as distant stars . . . .
Still, if I were called,
like the white streak of a comet
slicing through the veil of night,
I wouldn't freely go, even if
we are just bits of bright dust
slipping out of the pocket
of the dark . . . what more
do we know?

Moon light
etches the window glass—
the black and endless fields
stretch out above the oaks,
my father's ghost bumps
room to room.
   Yet a poem
comes sometimes in the middle
of the night, and something burns
in me clear and unafflicted.
I just hope it doesn't mean
I've used up most of my life
only to arrive here in the dark?
Always, I've wanted
to take the longest way around.
Like anyone, I have prayed
for a long life, but I have prayed
as resolutely for poems too.

SEPTEMBER

Light spliced through eucalyptus, strained
       through construction paper clouds
cut out and pinned over the eastern ridge—
       shorthand of leaves on the asphalt,
dry mist of grass spun over the playing field.
       A long drink from the water fountain,
last station wagon pulling out the gate,
       then we're walking home again
from childhood—doubling up on bikes, wind
       signing its name to everything
we take from the world on that ambered
       and soft angle of the air. . . .

No one comes back without that haze
       still settling in the heart,
without smoke brazing an afternoon
       of loquats and tangerines,
and the unvarying disposition of the space
       from the acacia to the oak
still empty, blue between my left hand
       and my right—though
I'm as far from any day you could name,
       burned or burning away
in the distributions of leaves or stars.
       Birds sing under

the rumor of rain, and we are walking
       ever closer to the past,
on that grey shore, electrons leaping above
       the glitter and delirium
of surf, the last small cloud bled of grace.

Here, beyond the sight of angels,
my lips taste of salt, chalk, and rust,
     of the raw skin of the sky
where a thin voice has called us back
     the whole time we've been
here, invisibly blessed, taking our every
     frivolous breath from the sea.

APOLOGIA PRO VITA SUA

Desertan los recuerdos en nube me memoria.
             —Luis Cernuda

It's still snowing forever in Washington Court House, Ohio, 1952—
      I've just picked up the *boule de neige* on my aunt's

knickknack table and shaken it to watch the soft flakes float down
      the watery air over the town . . . I have no explanation

for the past, for my unsubstantiated appraisals of the sea, for salt
      dried above my eyebrows like the membrane of a cloud,

the veiled physics of foam and spray disappearing on the California
      coast, coming to nothing on the air.   But the cold

equation of my breath reaches beyond the fading image of myself,
      beyond the improbable sky overhauled with the lost

composure of the stars. We arrive here, headed for the phylum of dust—
      clay tablets, scientific journals, palm pilots, no one thinks

they're going away empty-handed. I redeemed pop bottles for pennies,
      was transported into the shining realm of profit

and loss long before it all came to nothing but profit and loss, before
      everything escaped, momentarily fastened as it was

at ground level with a navy-blue school sweater tied around my waist,
      with gravity and oxygen as we looked up into the blue

every blessed day. My excuse has always been the depleted tune,
      the wages of the air, the anthem I sang tumbling

in the surf. All I have to contribute now is doubt, an initial public
    offering of depreciated metaphysical speculation—

the days paid out on the odds and ends of clouds—white blossoms, blank
    affidavits of belief. Longing hangs by every loose thread

of the wind, its choruses testifying hourly to all that's disappeared
    to an invisible frontier where the past is endless,

where I don't remember wanting much more than a baseball mitt and
    a pair of high-top PF flyers without holes in the bottoms,

where alone I saw a slant of light galvanized at the horizon's seam,
    attributing it to the soul, though it meant little

more than a thick glaze through palm fronds and pepper trees, dust
    the only evidence that a breeze sighed with meaning

through anything. What does it matter finally what I hope for? The Buddha
    said it's best to be empty, like a bowl, like a cloud, but

for all I know, the soul looks vacantly out its nine windows on stars
    washing up in the tide, dead stars, grey with time.

Nevertheless. We're left with a sky, a cloud, a soul, rose-white images
    recast and round with emptiness—these pelicans diving

and rising up from the sea, untroubled about their place on earth,
    who know the direction of Paradise as well as anyone . . . .

V

TRAVEL

I have never been to Buenos Aires or *Juan-les-Pins*
      for that matter, except in the dark

'40s and '50s films—and it was never Jean Seberg or
      Ingrid Bergman who ran up to me, shaking

the gold ocean from her short hair, looking into my eyes
      with all the lost minutes a black &white sea

withheld. Yet I recall the tangerine suns and sapphire
      lagoons on postcards of French Polynesia,

awash in junk shop drawers, and a lavish night sky
      over Yosemite, that deep blue table cloth

and the bread-crumb stars spinning evenly away from us
      toward a barricade of bright islands

we are never going to see. In this way, we received
      more darkness than light—the 10%

that escaped on the blast at the start, our souvenir
      of somewhere we've never been. Dreamers,

walkers in our easy sleep, we unfolded our arms and
      filled them with the lost destinations,

the local outskirts of the air, with the last image of the sea
      which compares us to clouds under sail,

in transit to who knows where. Sundown, and the shore
    birds head homeward with the song

that first pulled them away—the sky, like everything,
    still unresolved. You can hear the dark

rustling overhead, the sky we can never return to, empty-
    handed as we are with only our obvious

hearts as guide. Any way you look at it, it's a long way
    to go to have only come this far.

THE PHILOSOPHY PROFESSOR FACING RETIREMENT

Don't beg.
—Carlos Drummond de Andrade

The sky leaning on your shoulders, scuffed as it was
    left—and you're still free to breathe,
        but stand here as long as you can,

there is no breath of God, only the misplaced pages
    of the wind with no further elaboration
        of the beginning or the end, and,

as likely as not, you were given everything you deserved—
    a yard, youth flaming like the oranges there,
        rain abstract among the leaves,

but reasonable corroboration for the ontological trees,
    beyond which, you have found little cause
        to look. The sea's chilled affection

remains your one tangible award—the past glazing
    your tongue with an ineffective fury. Gusts
        in the side streets continue

to make the case that we are all foundlings beneath the self-
    sufficient clouds, and will, with impartiality,
        see similar ends no matter

what knowledge we were refused. Light or darkness escapes
    the clogged and paradigmatic stars—time is not up,
        but we look done for with as much

irony as melancholy cresting on white caps and the waves,
    or in clouds again, grim bridges to the end,
        all our portraits hanging in the gallery

of dusk. Joy—for all empirical purposes—was spread so thin
as to admit only a few hermits into the hypothesis.
You know the stars are not thorns

in some introspective sky, just particle streams, wavy packets
of light, blown about, harmless unless you recall
those over your blue childhood,

that night when the heavens took their place . . . . Now and then,
off-white and amber clouds float over from Italy,
billowing almost beatifically with belief . . .

but the term's almost up, you're late home on the local bus,
car in the shop awaiting parts. First evening star
that's not really a star, last petticoat

narcissus by the children's stickmen chalked on the wall—
there is no connection. A neighbor's leaves blow
across your lawn with little consequence . . .

on the porch, no paper, no dog to greet you with a limping
faith—and even if you had one now, you'd kick it,
for no reason you'll ever know.

TELEOLOGY

All the hoboes have gone to their rewards,
    skin like paper grocery bags,
        maps crumpled against heaven . . .

The rest of us are still working things out,
    simple instruments, industrious occasions
        of cause and effect.

If I overlook all that has come to me outside of reason
    and that first consequence of design, I see
        I've offered my purest affections

to the past, where, it seemed, there was a mind
    external to the orbits of the spheres.
        Now, beside the watery skein

of evening, I'm sitting on the inevitable sands
    of melancholy, sifting that salt and
        sweetness I left behind

long ago, for reasons that completely escape me. Yet
    the sea wants nothing from me, demands
        less than when I supposed

it represented invisible origins—divine retribution
    in storm surf and rip tides that pulled
        the cliffs and earth away.

My version of the sky, unlike the sun-colored oriole's,
    is inconsolable and will not stand up
        as the dark moves in,

the analogous bird seed of the galaxies and stars
     scattered indiscriminately in every direction.
        For any evidence I've come across,

God has kept to himself—and I've been left with a jumble
     of clouds to decipher—loaves and fishes, feathers
        off the angels' empty plates.

Foundling of days, my days floated above the waves
     where I could not see to the source
        of anything beyond the fusion

of oxygen into the salt lanes of my unremitting blood.
     Here is my soul, driftwood beached up
        along side the midday moon

and the ice-colored clouds that never look away
     from confusion. The white sky
        turns grey, and nothing

I know will, in the end, save me from Nothing,
     if that's what's there. I catch myself
        looking up, talking out loud

to the house finch and crowned sparrow in
     the Brisbane Box. And if it turns out
        we were intended for something

beyond utility all along, then I will be reproved,
     and will find my place among the everlasting
        and glittering particulate of space . . . .

PROHECY

and who are they

their wings horizon edged

—Charles Wright

White, immemorial sky, salt glaze
over the orchard,

the untitled loss the daylight and I
have been rehearsing

among the lemon leaves, the exhalation
of evening moving

through us by degrees with its blue
jigsaw of stars . . .

each moment in the universe burning
away, railroaded

on cold light, where, for the time being,
we hold off

our programmed obsolescence, circling
the crosswords of dust.

★

Such an unmendable light, unbearable
over the quiet road

we keep looking down for all those
we've known to come

walking back to us in their old coats
and bones—a little

like clouds comfortable in their maisonettes,
        but whatever lifts

back like water to the sky has been
        beyond me.

Salvation . . . how is that going
        to happen here?

★

In a café, in an empty bar, a jukebox
        is still spinning

45s from the '50s, and somewhere
        above Texas

or New Mexico Les Paul & Mary Ford
        are still singing

"Vaya Con Dios, My Darling" in amplified,
        reverberated harmonies,

as close as we're likely to get, this side,
        to the other . . . .

★

I sit down to remember the days, to sift
        the grey powder

of the past through my stiff fingers
        a while, never knowing

why we've been arguing all this time
        over the life

we've received. And when the rain
    arrives tonight

across the San Rafaels, the faces I see,
    or the dark leaves

falling, will have nothing to tell me,
    and I will act

as if it's something new again, though
    I have yet to hear

a single *grito* from the void—though that is
    not absolutely essential

to our case. On nights like these, a fingernail
    is often run along

the electric edge of the horizon
    just to keep us

in doubt about everything
    around us—

the bell-clappered air, the cracks
    in the sea

unraveling when the afternoon is finished
    and I look out

and know that soon, there will be no one
    who ever knew us.

ENTROPY

Sooner or later a time comes
When it's all the same
Whether you talk or not,
So you might as well shut up.
—Alfredo, *Cinema Paradiso*

The stars above home shone like little pats
    Of butter across the blue face

Of Paradise, like the glitter off silverware
    In those '50s supper clubs—

Frozen back there, complete in your eyes,
    When you could barely say

The names for things. You spoke your first
    Words of French 50 years ago,

Though you were not destined for the diplomatic
    Core or 5-Star restaurants

On the Champs-Elysées. Like Latin, you parsed
    And diagramed, you decoded

That portion of the sky that held its place
    Over the harbor and the shore,

Over the Limbo of the sea—everything becoming
    Incrementally unclear, with

No one really, turning a hand beyond
    The expected historical

Catastrophes, singing of arms and men again . . . .
How easily the past continues

To lose itself in the wilderness of the sea—
Amphorae, silver plate, beads.

The unwearied eloquence of the waves continues
To outstrip anything I have

To contribute, but that, too, will give way
To the held cosmic breath,

When our atmosphere unravels and the last
Atom of mist lifts off

To become nothing again. My mind is a cloud,
And a little wind sometimes,

An afterthought of order moving through it.
Clouds are phrased together, mute

Syllables of light unstrung, years gone by,
Measureless in the sun . . . .

The earliest Chinese writings were divinations
Scratched on tortoise shells

And the shoulder bones of cattle—grey
Hexagrams, asterisks, smudges

We can now no more surely interpret
Than the quasars arriving

Out of the blue—15 billion years old—on
Our stellar photo plates.

The 2nd Law of Thermodynamics tells us that
    Everything dissipates in the end,

That all messages decay with time and distance—
    If in fact there was a message

And it was anything more than time and distance . . . .
    Behind the olive trees, a wind

Reiterates the inadequate arrangements of hope.
    The light is lying down, edging

Toward winter, and heaven looks cold from here.
    Finally, I think, my dust is not

Going to chorus the praises of creation, and if God
    Were sitting on the next bench over,

Taking in the evening air, turning over recent
    developments in the dark,

I would not go over and try to bum a smoke,
    mention offhand the obvious

Contradiction of evil in the world. It's too late
    For that theocratic spin and

Dodge; I wouldn't want to further bore us both.
    No, I'd ask about the hard science

Of dirt and decay, the charge and small change
    Of chemicals we come out to.

And oh yes—the music of the spheres—where
    Did that fly off to, leaving us

With only a faint red hum, microwave of that
    Molecular sea-flat blast

Beneath each stone or leaf? And how did he
    Work it out so we could turn

Back all the pages of the light, but never read
    To the beginning, and be left over-

Looking the ocean at a point where we would
    Finally be content to fill a silence,

Just whistling into a breeze, with the last
    Atoms of our worthless breath.

THE UNCERTAINTY PRINCIPLE

The stars above us actually aren't . . .
they're just pin-balled
every which way, pitching about
in the galactic swill—scads of them
like pebbles the ocean drags back
in its moon-tide and ebb.

      Our atoms
no different, derived from theirs,
shining until we likewise are
decompressed with time
and float out to darkness.

      At least
we think it's Time we're looking at
out there as we add our short run up
and develop our takes on nebulae
still popping like '50s flash bulbs ,
paparazzi of death at the far end
of any lens, despite whatever zoom out
to deep distance or wide-angle,
the fish-eye of the infinite.

      Quasars,
missing matter, black holes—variables
of a cosmic throw of the dice—amino acids,
salt water and a comet's hodgepodge of filched
chemicals that have consciousness
rising like steam off a primordial soup—
who can do the math, the likelihood
of mammals advancing upright
over the grassy planes ?

      The past
contains everything—red-shifted
like a freight train speeding off
into Kansas, bringing the near and far

loss of childhood home each night,
and each of us equally impoverished in that.
Yet everything else is still
going to happen somewhere—so what
are we to believe?
How then
does Heisenberg's Principle—
the mechanical quantum sophistry—
help us? By his own admission,
it's impossible to determine
the speed and location
of an object because energy
and momentum are exchanged
just looking, and this spoils
the original details of the system.
The laws of cause and effect then
don't apply, but in 1932
they gave him the Nobel anyway.
Perhaps the reductive analogy helps:
whatever is observed is changed
by the observation. How then
will our true natures, let alone
the light-clogged patterns
of other galaxies—ever be known,
if God—as Sister Caritas proclaimed
on the first day of school—is in fact
watching us?
So here I am,
evening coming in, the sky
staggering off through the trees,
and I feel as artless as the air,
my mind's unsteady thoughts
blowing around, straw in a breeze . . . .
I have no idea how far
these few clouds will get

across the sky. I've rounded off
clouds to the nearest zero,
but have lost count on the high,
blackboard of the blue—
most likely I should ask nothing
of anything beyond the air,
given how much evidence
has escaped us.
                    Each day
the clouds enter a new world,
never what they were, every
anecdote and historical bit
of us they've overlooked, scattered
like flash-cards and left
behind them.
                    You offer one reason
or another—the earth is made
of fire, or air, or water, rarefied
and condensed—of leptons, muons,
or quarks, left handed, right handed
or charmed, and what reason
has the sky to listen?
                    Nobody
asked you. Each evening brings
to mind all the still space where
we are not—and even with the first
underestimated equation of the seas
to fall back on, the formulas
for splendor seem to be random,
unaccounted for, and few.

COMPLICITY—APRIL 21, 2004

> To die man has no need of God.
> But God needs men in order to live.
> —Luis Cernuda

I long ago gave in
         to evening's blue hum edging the palisades
                like the after-flutter
of a ballad note
         from Ben Webster's tenor sax—
            sun, red as a blood-spot on an egg,
and soon,
     at my fingertips,
          the white stars again
              lifting away—
                 nothing keeps its place.

He knew we'd eventually
         get an angle on it,
              resourcefully
as our genes were engineered.
        But always too late to act
             on our knowledge—
thin as our speculative skins,
        the jellied cosmic light
            and first blue note
of time or space,
        the invisible ink
             of the universe.
          And so 50 or more years into it,
we've launched a missile with gyroscopes
            precise enough
              to test
Einstein's theories

about the fundamental equations
                          and relative facts
of God,
      and report back
            with the abbreviated view from here,
                              the synecdoche
of our souls,
            the dissolution of the molecular template,
                              bones and blueprints
we continue to develop outside
                  of any scientific guarantees.

                        The more astrophysics
we are exposed to,
            the more likely we are to believe anything.
                        Some one dreamed up
divine abstractions, the body politic,
            with nothing finally
                        more incontestable,
than the sand flies in their black galaxies
                        about the rotting kelp.

God, so it seems, requires our support
                        above the discursive tides,
the proletarian stars.
            I only offer up this green water,
                              the salt
and spare sweetness.
            Just above the power lines,
                        the brown atmosphere—
He must have been sick at heart
                  all this time,
                        and only left us

the abandoned stations
of the clouds
as sign posts,
as pale metaphysical suffixes
sketched over
the switchbacks of sorrow.
If it turns out that we were
in paradise all along,
then I will have
wasted my time complaining
about the conditional data—
the oceans,
nevertheless, sparing us nothing
of the old longing—
the dust-blue
horizon going dark,
in concert,
as foretold—
one more hostage among us.

ABOUT THE AUTHOR

Christopher Buckley has published fourteen books of poetry, most recently, *Sky* (The Sheep Meadow Press, 2004) and *Star Apocrypha* (Northwestern Univ. Press, 2001). For his poetry he has received four Pushcart Prizes, two awards from the Poetry Society of America, a Fulbright Award in Creative Writing to the former Yugoslavia, and is the recipient of NEA grants in poetry for 2001 and 1984.

Buckley is the editor of a number of anthologies of contemporary poetry as well as critical books about contemporary poets and poetry. Most recently he has edited *Homage to Vallejo* (Greenhouse Review Press, 2006), and *A Condition of the Spirit: The Life and Work of Larry Levis* (Eastern Washington Univ. Press, 2004, with Alexander Long). With Gary Young, Buckley is the editor of *The Geography of Home: California's Poetry of Place* (Hey Day Books, 1999), and with David Oliveira and M.L. Williams he is editor of *How Much Earth: The Fresno Poets* (Round House Press, 2001). For the University of Michigan Press' Under Discussion Series, he has edited *The Poetry of Philip Levine: Stranger to Nothing,* 1991.

In 2001, Buckley published *Appreciations: Selected Reviews, Views, and Interviews 1975-2000*, and his first book of creative nonfiction, *Cruising State: Growing Up in California* was published in 1994 by the Univ. of Nevada Press. A new book of nonfiction, *Sleep Walk,* will be published by the Eastern Washington Univ. Press in 2006.